AF211748

D.L. CRAYVER

BUDGET TRAVELERS

The Ultimate Guide to Traveling on a Budget, Learn the Secrets and Best Practices on How you Can Have The Best Travel Experience on a Small Budget

Descrierea CIP a Bibliotecii Naţionale a României
D.L. CRAYVER
    BUDGET TRAVELERS. The Ultimate Guide to Traveling on a Budget, Learn the Secrets and Best Practices on How you Can Have The Best Travel Experience on a Small Budget / D.L. Crayver – Bucharest: Editura My Ebook, 2020
    ISBN

D.L. CRAYVER

BUDGET TRAVELERS

The Ultimate Guide to Traveling on a Budget, Learn the Secrets and Best Practices on How you Can Have The Best Travel Experience on a Small Budget

My Ebook Publishing House
Bucharest, 2020

TABLE OF CONTENTS

INTRODUCTION

Traveling is seen as a luxury that can be afforded only by some and necessitates saving over several months in order to get the holiday that you want. This does not have to be the case. With a bit of careful thought and a lot of planning, it really is possible to travel on a budget.

Of course, traveling on a budget means different things to different people. Some would consider a budget holiday to involve backpacking and camping. This type of holiday can be done on a budget relatively easily; the real skill arises when you are trying to get a 'luxury' holiday for a budget price.

The Travel Industry Association of America estimated that the average family spends over 2,200 a year on an extended vacation. This is an enormous amount. If you save just 10% of that amount, think how it will add up over the years.

Interestingly, paying more does not necessarily guarantee you a better holiday. Whenever you are on vacation, you will probably be surrounded by other families, some of which have paid more than you for the vacation and others which have paid significantly less.

This book is all about learning to be one of those who sits smugly by the others declaring the 'cheap' vacation that they have managed to secure. It's easier than you think!

1. PLANNING YOUR VACATION

Planning is the key to success when it comes to getting a budget holiday. There are many things that you can influence such as when you book, how you travel, whether you go package or build your own agenda. All of these things can have a significant impact on the price you pay. Above all, each of these things are within your control!

1.1. When to Book

Most people know exactly when they are intending to take a vacation. This can be used to your advantage when it comes to planning.

Deciding on when to book is a bit of a gamble. Whilst many tour operators will offer cheaper prices and early booking discounts, you may find that last minute deals are also available which will prove better financially.

There are many factors that you should take into account when deciding on when to book for maximum financial gain:

- Are you flexible in terms of dates that you are prepared to travel?

- Are you flexible in terms of destinations that you are prepared to travel to?

- Will you be buying a package deal or will you be building your own package?

- Are you considering a popular destination where many tour operators or flight companies travel?

Firstly, if you are flexible in terms of location and dates then you will almost certainly benefit from waiting until the last minute to book your holiday. Last minute deals are, of course, something that you cannot rely upon and if you are set on going to a certain destination at a certain date then last minute is far too risky.

If you are planning on creating your own package then you need to be aware that you are taking multiple gambles. For example, you need to consider your airfare, hotels and transport. Whilst you may get an excellent last minute flight, you may not be so lucky when it comes to the hotel or car hire. In fact, you may find that paying a premium for other parts of your holiday will end up out-weighing any last minute savings you have made.

As a general rule, if you are looking to go on a specific holiday, a cruise, for example, with a specific company or a destination that is only offered by a few operators, you may find that last minute bargains are simply not available. Cruising is a classic example of this. A cruise line will offer holidays for a certain price, whilst they may offer their holidays through different agents who may individually offer discounts, the actual price of the cruise is likely to remain very similar no matter who you go to for your price.

2. CHOOSING YOUR SEASON
AND DESTINATION

The two key things that can have a huge impact on the cost of your vacation are the destination and the time of year. In fact, the single biggest saver is likely to be when you travel, not how successfully you manage to haggle for that last minute hotel bargain!

Don't overlook the importance of considering these two factors together. Some destinations will be extremely cheap at one time of year yet finding a bargain four months later may be impossible. Traveling to a popular destination at a peak time will never be cheap. For example staying at a luxury hotel in a party city on New Year's Eve is not likely to be a budget holiday; however, traveling to a traditional summer resort over New Year's may be a very different story.

One thing that is very important to realize is that low seasons are low for a reason. A classic example of this is hurricane season in the Caribbean and Florida. Other low seasons to be wary of are the extremely hot areas such as Egypt during the summer months, when the heat can be so oppressive that it makes the holiday less enjoyable. Summer resorts are often so quiet during low season that there is quite literally nowhere open. This can be great for a retreat, but when it comes to a raging nightlife you may be sadly disappointed!

2.1. Shoulder Season

Shoulder season is the perfect time to be trying to travel for those who want to find a happy medium between low and peak seasons. Identifying where is in shoulder season when you want to travel or when your favorite destination is in shoulder season can save you literally hundreds of dollars.

Take a look at the guide books. Whilst they will not tell you when the shoulder season is, they will tell you when peak and low seasons are. The time in between, is, by definition, the shoulder season.

With almost every resort there is a period where the prices become low, not because the location is now poor but because all of the hotels and flights are still servicing the area but the demand is simply not there. Examples of shoulder seasons are Europe in the fall and the Caribbean during late spring.

2.2. Winter

Winter is an interesting time of year to travel. Before Christmas, most individuals are trying to make last minute shopping trips. After Christmas, people are dealing with their credit card bills. As such, holidays on far off beaches are often incredibly cheap during the winter period.

A wonderful destination for the winter months is Asia. Flights are losing popularity, however, availability is still good, meaning that there are plenty of discounts on offer. Weather is variable in Asia during the winter which could mean that you are surrounded by snow one minute and then basking in glorious sunshine. This lack of dependability is something that puts a lot of visitors off and can mean that there are some excellent bargains for those prepared to take the risk!

2.3. Spring

If you are looking to travel to Europe, this is the time to do it! Flights are a lot cheaper during the spring months when temperatures are still relatively low.

Mexican beaches and the Caribbean islands start to see their prices drop from mid April as the weather becomes hotter. However, during the spring months, the water and air temperatures are still pleasant and the resorts less crowded.

During later spring, for example May, the traditionally hot and dry countries are not in their peak seasons but have not yet become intolerably hot. So if you want to visit Morocco, Jordan or Egypt, plan a spring vacation.

2.4. Summer

Finding a bargain in summer is tricky. Americans, Japanese and Europeans are all on the move and this is also the time of year that most weddings take place, so honeymoon destinations are in a great deal of demand.

During the early part of summer, through June and July, Caribbean destinations are still good to get a deal, provided you try to book before the Europeans start to flood in during their school holidays at the end of July.

Safari holidays are a good option between June and September. High season ends in May, but the weather is still relatively dry.

Flights and hotels are still quite reasonable in Southeast Asia during the summer months, but temperatures can be quite hot, so if you can't stand the heat, avoid this destination during the summer months.

2.5. Fall

This is the time to head to Europe. Flights to most major European destinations will be cheaper from October onwards, mainly because the schools are no longer on holiday and families are not traveling as much. Temperatures are normally perfectly pleasant until mid November, so grab yourself a fall bargain in Europe.

3. HOTELS AT LAST MINUTE

For the brave, it is always worth calling the hotel that you want to stay at on the day that you intend to arrive, or possibly the day before. Hotels will often be prepared to offer substantial discounts on the day, as from their point of view an empty room is a complete waste of money. If you are feeling particularly bold it is even worth telling the hotel what you are prepared to pay and asking them if they have any rooms available.

This is a particularly effective way of going about getting a really good deal if you are traveling to a city that has several hotels, it is out of peak season and you are flexible in terms of facilities.

If you are not feeling quite so bold in terms of leaving it until the last minute, you can phone the hotel a few days in advance. Whilst you may not get the total bargains, you are still in a good position to negotiate, particularly if you are traveling out of season. If you are targeting a specific hotel, check out

17

their cancellation policy. For example, if a specific hotel requires at least 3 days notice to not charge for a cancellation, then this is the point where they are most likely to receive the most cancellations. Hotels will then be eager to fill these spaces.

Another good way to utilize the cancellation policies of hotels is to book a relatively cheap chain hotel that allows you to cancel free up until the day of travel. Then, on the day you can phone around other hotels to see if you can get a better deal. If you do then you can cancel your previous booking without penalty; if you do not then you will still have a roof over your head!

Negotiations over extra free nights or discounts will generally only work with smaller regional hotels, as the larger chains have a central system and they will not normally negotiate directly with a guest. Bear this in mind when you are selecting your targets!

Facilities such as swimming pools, fitness centers, satellite televisions all add to the costs of a hotel. Consider this carefully. Are you paying extra for facilities that you don't want, won't need and don't even notice? If you are after a cheap base, then avoid hotels with extra facilities as this will almost invariably add to your costs.

4. BAGGING A CHEAP FLIGHT

Buying a last minute flight is actually quite tricky. Many charter airlines will deal primarily with packages and as such the flight-only option can actually end up costing more than a simple package.

All is not lost though! There are still plenty of ways to pick up a flight bargain. Bear in mind that if you are going for a do it yourself option on your holiday, it is wise to book the flight first, as this is likely to be the largest expenditure and there is generally less of a variety of carriers meaning less room for negotiation. Almost without exception finding a cheap hotel will be easier than finding a cheap flight.

Trawl the websites of those flight operators that cover the location which you wish to travel to. Join their mailing list. OK, so you may end up with endless junk mail, but you will also get to hear about all of the deals that they are currently offering.

As a general rule, the best deals are available for flights leaving Monday to Thursday and on domestic flights many bargains can be found on a Saturday. Travelers will almost invariably pay more for a Friday or Sunday flight. Most holiday operators will offer the best deals for those who purchase a set time in advance, normally at least 14 days. If it is possible to stay a Saturday night, this will also normally result in a lower fare.

When searching, if possible, entertain the possibility of a flight that involves a connection. Airlines often place a large premium on non-stop flights and if this is not vital for you, you are likely to be able to save many dollars.

A further premium is normally placed on 'nice' flight times, i.e. ones that will not involve a particularly early start or involve traveling over night. Again if you are prepared to compromise slightly on your flight times, you may find that you can make huge savings.

Try not to stick rigidly to your destination. It may be possible to fly into a nearby airport and drive the last hour or so; this may offer you a better price overall.

Whenever you are considering buying a flight, it is always worth going to a consolidator such as Orbitz or Expedia. This will give you some excellent background information, such as the operators that offer the destination you are after and the typical prices. By doing your homework you will be able to act quickly when you see a bargain in the future. Very good deals often only appear for a very short period of time so it is important that you learn to recognize a good deal so that you can pounce on one-off deals before they disappear. When you are doing your homework, try a search with 'flexible dates'. This will allow you to get a good feel for the price differences that are in operation during your ideal travel period.

A few other hints that can help you to bag a flight bargain is to consider air courier travel. To be able to become a courier you will have to be very flexible, prepared to travel alone with very little luggage, but on the plus side you will get to travel to new places very cheaply.

Some countries offer air passes to tourists that allow discounts if you are planning on spending a lot of time traveling around a particular region such as Australia or Europe.

If you book an airline ticket and then find that the price has gone down, contact the airline and ask for a refund. Many of the large airlines offer to pay back the difference if the prices go down. Read the small print and ask for the refund if it applies. Even if your chosen airline does not offer this sort of refund policy it is still worth asking as with increased competition airlines are very keen to keep customers happy.

5. BARGAIN PACKAGE HOLIDAYS

Package holidays are simply holidays where the travel operator offers the whole trip, including the flights, hotels and in some cases the transport when you arrive at your destination. Bearing this in mind, a lot of the tips for getting cheap flights will be the same as they are for package holidays. Having said this, there are some specific ways of bagging a package holiday bargain.

The reason that many tour operators offer such cheap deals for packages is because they buy a certain number of flights and hotel rooms which they then try and sell throughout the year. By definition, they will have more possible holidays during peak season, but then there will also be greater demand meaning that the bargains may not be what you would hope.

Last minute package holidays are readily available if you are not fussy about destination and can wait until the very last minute. If you simply want somewhere hot, tomorrow, you will almost certainly bag a bargain; if you want a specific type of destination or resort then you may find that you are not able to get that last minute deal.

Optional extras are big business for package tour operators and they will often make most of their profit from these extras such as insurance, excursions and transport at your destination. Whilst these will often be available elsewhere cheaper, you may find that purchasing these from your package holiday operator will allow you to negotiate a discount on your holiday. You may even be able to get a 'free' extra if you agree to book on the spot.

Another thing to bear in mind is that accommodation is not the expensive part of the package and you will sometimes find that a package holiday to a particular destination will end up as a cheaper alternative to trying to book flights on their own. Last minute package deals are often so cheap that you can take the point of view that even if you hate the accommodation you can always phone around for your chosen hotel. On a similar note, the best bargains are often those that are classified as 'allocation on arrival'. This simply means that you will be allocated accommodation when you arrive.

Some operators offer a halfway option where you will be told the resort, the type of hotel or the grade but the final selection will be done when you arrive.

6. SPECIALIST BARGAINS

Adventure travel has always been regarded as the expensive option. This need not be the case, although adventure tour operators invariably are expensive as they pay developed world prices to their sales, marketing and organizational staff.

If you consider a typical adventure holiday, you will find that only a minimal portion of the overall cost will end up going on the actual adventure part of the holiday. By organizing your own trip directly, you could save literally thousands of dollars.

Booking an adventure holiday for yourself can be quite tricky so follow these guidelines to make sure you get it right!

- Word of mouth is invaluable when you are considering going off the beaten track. If you can find someone that you know who has done your trip before, you may be able to get some excellent tips on what to do

- Get hold of a couple of guidebooks on the areas that you are considering. Whilst travel book writers may vary in opinions, any underlying themes should be taken seriously!

- Look at message boards online. The internet is a superb resource and will allow you to contact many people who have first hand experience of your destination.

- If you are going on a guided tour once you reach your destination, make sure that you get everything straight before you depart. Ensure that you discuss with your guide what is included and what is not. Agree a price before you leave as you will be in a much weaker position once you are halfway up a mountain!

Generally booking a tour once you arrive at your destination will mean that you get a better deal. However, this will not work if you are traveling to a very tight schedule, want to do a specific route or you do not speak the local language. In these cases it is would normally be worth booking from home before you travel.

6.1. Round the World

Traveling around the world may be the last thing on your mind if you are looking for a budget holiday. However, bear in mind that once you are on the move, the incremental cost of an extra stop will not be as large as the cost of traveling that destination from home on a different occasion.

Many operators will also often offer a discount for travelers who want to make several stops, so if you really fancy a couple of nights en-route, enquire about options. You may be pleasantly surprised.

Another possible option is to simply book a one way ticket to your first destination, this will allow you the flexibility to decide when you want to travel on, and will also allow you to benefit from buying locally, which will almost invariably mean you get cheaper rate. One of the main disadvantages of this method is that you are in effect stranded and if you cannot find a cheap flight, you will have to buy one anyway! Immigration officers are also a little more fussy when it comes to admitting someone only with a one way ticket and no obvious onward plans.

6.2. Cruise Bargains

Very few people ever pay the full brochure price for a cruise. This is a fact, so getting a discount from the advertised prices should be relatively easy.

One thing that visitors should consider with cruises is that you are going to be on board this ship for the duration of your holiday. It is not like a package holiday where if you dislike the resort you can simply leave; here you are captive. If you love the ship this is wonderful, if you hate it is the holiday from hell.

The first thing you should do once you have narrowed down the cruise liners that you are interested in, is to look at what prices the cruise lines themselves are offering the holidays for. This will give you an idea of when you are facing a bargain.

Last minute bargains are few and far between on cruises, so do not rely on this in the same way that you would for a flight or hotel.

When it comes to cruising, finding a specialist travel agent will normally be a good move. Contact suitable looking agents and ask to be put on their mailing list. If you are interested in a specific line or destination make this known to them.

There are also plenty of websites such as CruiseMates that have a bargain finder, where you can say what you are looking forward and agents will then contact you with the best deal.

Another thing to bear in mind is that children often pay full adult price on cruises if they are taking a full adult berth. Look out for child-specific deals if they share your cabin. Some cruise lines offer the option of booking a cabin grade but not a specific cabin. This will often mean that if they have spare space you are upgraded to the next grade or even beyond. Of course the down side is that you could end up in one of the worst cabins of the grade that you have paid for.

Cruise lines like to keep their customers and many lines will offer you incentives to book for the following year when you are onboard. Typically you can expect to get a decent amount of money as onboard credit which will mean that you get the benefit of your early booking next year. Most lines also offer loyalty programs, so enquire about these on board, too.

7. WHERE TO LOOK

7.1. Introduction

Having decided that you want your bargain holiday, you now have to turn your attention to starting your search. Knowing where to look for the bargains is the main part of the battle when it comes to securing that extra special deal.

Traditionally, travelers would only really be able to use local agents to deal with their query. These days however we have a wealth of options available to us including online consolidators, auction sites and direct web sites to peruse.

Deciding on the best place to look will depend on a number of factors such as where you are going, when you are going, whether you need any specialist advice and how much leg work you want to put in yourself.

In reality the best option will be to consult several different sources, even if it is simply to be certain that you are getting the best possible deal from your chosen retailer.

7.2. Auction sites

Auction sites are a relatively new concept and one that has still not reached its full potential. Many people are still wary about the concept of bidding for a holiday. One of the most popular auction sites that is used at the moment is eBay; however, bidders should be aware that they are often buying from an individual and the motto 'buyer beware' could not be any more appropriate. However, if you browse through eBay you may find that a lot of the tour operators advertise their deals on eBay in a clearance type of fashion. If you do not wish to purchase through eBay, this still gives you a good idea of the types of prices that agents are prepared to let the holidays go for. Similarly, hotels often advertise any spare capacity that they have on sites such as eBay and this can be a great way to pick up a bargain.

There are also sites that are dedicated to auctioning holidays such as biddingfortravel.com, where companies offer their availability and the hotel, flight, or holiday is simply sold to the highest bidder. The real danger with this type of purchase is that it is normally allocation on arrival or limited in terms of options. Auction sites are a great place to look if you are very flexible, however, if you want a specific destination, date or other parameter, think twice! Another thing to bear in mind is that many of the auction sites will add an extra fee on to your winning price, so check out any extras that you will be expected to pay so that you do not get any nasty shocks.

Also if you are traveling in a family group, bear in mind that prices normally reflect double occupancy only and the hotel in question may not be able to accommodate children in the same room. Check these details out BEFORE you bid, as any bid you make is binding.

7.3. Travel Agent

Many people have speculated that traditional travel agents are a dying breed as more travelers start to build their own packages. To a certain extent this is true; however, travel agents still have a very valuable role to play in helping travelers to locate a bargain.

A registered travel agency will have necessary insurance so that if something happens to mean that you do not get the holiday that you booked, you will receive some compensation. This security may be particularly important if you are booking a very important holiday such as a honeymoon

Smaller agents also will have a greater discretion than large online chains. When you purchase online you are usually told the price; there is no room to negotiate for extras or further discounts.

By dealing with a person in a face-to-face situation, you are in a much stronger position to negotiate.

A holiday is only a bargain if you get the holiday that you will enjoy. If you are looking at a specialist holiday type, such as a cruise, then an experienced travel agent will be extremely valuable to ensure that you get the best possible holiday. True you are likely to pay a little extra for this level of expertise, but it is not worth saving a few dollars at the expense of your enjoyment.

Building up a rapport with a travel agent will mean that they personally keep you in mind and if requested, they will be able to notify of you of any potentially interesting bargains that come into their agency, before they are released to the public. They may also be aware of any upcoming sales that are not generally public knowledge. If you have had a cheap quote online, take the details into your local agent and ask them what they can do, you may be pleasantly surprised!

7.4. Online Purchases

Let's face it; most of us looking for a travel bargain will start their search online. Over the last few years online travel sites have gone from strength to strength. Travelocity, for example, has only been around for 10 years; last year it made a total of $830 million and took $7.4 billion worth of bookings.

Booking online has become incredibly popular; in 2005, 79 million people in the United States made their travel plans online. With so many people going online to book their holidays, it is little wonder that competition between the online agencies is reaching fever pitch. The good news is that a savvy consumer can use this to their advantage.

7.5. Consolidators

Companies such as Orbitz, Travelocity and Expedia are among the best known sites available for online purchases. One of the great benefits of these sites is that they cover the whole spectrum of options and often offer discounts on hotels and flights booked together. These are a great place to start the bargain hunt as they will alert you to the airlines that cover certain areas and will also tell you which flight times are the cheapest.

At the time of going to press, there is not one consolidator that covers ALL of the airlines. For this reason, it is likely that you will have to go to several sites before you are able to get a true picture of the bargains that are available.

Other sites such as priceline.com and hotwire.com will often offer enormous bargains. However, they do not always tell you whom exactly your booking is with until it is too late. Therefore, if you have a preference in terms of airline or hotel, these sites are not likely to be the best option for you.

Many of the consolidator websites are affiliated to a particular airline. Check out any affiliations that your chosen site may have, as this may have an effect on what they offer to the customer.

Buying online is often the cheapest way to get a holiday. However, bear in mind that as a rule, complicated requests or specific holidays will be better booked through a traditional agent who can offer the safety net and expertise that you desire.

8. MONEY SAVING TIPS

8.1. Introduction

As well as the usual ways to get a bargain flight or holiday, it is also important to consider other money saving tips for when you are actually traveling. Money saving tips whilst you are away should not be overlooked, as they can save you a substantial amount of money in the long run.

Another issue that you should consider before booking is what potential specialist discounts you may be entitled to; for example, many agents offer discounts to students, seniors or individuals that are members of certain organizations may also be able to get better deals.

When it comes to student travel you may find that the discounts are available for anyone aged 26 or under, regardless of whether they are actually students. If you are a student or under 26 then contact the specialist student agents such as

Student Universe, STA and Council Travel to find out what deals they have available.

Similarly there are specialist deals for seniors find out which of the airlines you are considering offer discounts for AARP members. If you are getting a senior rate you may find that your companion can also benefit from the same rate. Be sure to ask about these rates and any coupons or vouchers that are offered to senior travelers.

8.2. Clubs and Award Programs

Being a member of an airline or hotel awards program is a superb way of finding out about the bargains and also for making ongoing savings every time you travel. As a general rule there is no limit to the number of award programs that you can join, but normally you will have to decide which of the award programs you wish to assign any points you earn during a vacation.

Frequent Flyer Points

Large airline companies now offer frequent flier incentives as a matter of course. Take some time to locate the best deal based on your own individual circumstances. As well as gaining points every time you fly you can also become part of a mailing list that ensures you are notified of the hot deals of the day!

The largest frequent flyer programs in America are United's Mileage Plus, Delta's SkyMiles and American's Aadvantage. On average they have 20 million members each.

Hotel Award Programs

Hotel chains are keen to ensure that they have loyal customers and as such the larger chains will almost always offer some incentive for repeat bookings. Always ask what incentives are available, particularly if you can't choose between two different hotels. If one offers a good ongoing program, this may sway your decision. Some of the more popular offerings include a free upgrade if you stay for 10 days over the course of a year, free nights, free wine in your room.

Holiday Inn was the first hotel chain to begin to offer incentives and in the early days it was an impressive offer! After 75 days stay a traveler would get 2 airline tickets to Europe! Needless to say, this program was popular but soon had to be discontinued due to the amount it was costing the company. They do now have a very good awards program, just not quite as generous!

Combined Award Programs

Although some hotels and airlines offer frequent flyer points that encourage you to use their specific company, these sometimes will not offer you the best deal in combination. There are now plenty of companies that allow you to gather points whenever you use transport or goods that are affiliated to awards company.

Affiliates can be anything from hotels and flights to restaurants and clothing. Joining is normally easy and free, and with a bit of careful planning can yield huge rewards. What have you got to lose?

9. SAVING MONEY WHEN YOU ARE AT YOUR DESTINATION

When traveling independently you will almost always do better in terms of price and quality if you veer away from the traditional places to eat and shops that the guide books mention. Going off the beaten track can mean you pick up a real bargain.

9.1. Restaurants

Follow the locals; if you head for a tourist orientated restaurant or shop you will find that the prices are substantially higher and often the food is not of the same quality.

Another good tip is to visit the local market where the locals shop. Not only will you get fresh products at good prices but you will also enjoy the experience of mixing with the locals. Ask those around you where to go, after all, it is the locals that are best placed to tell you where to go for a good deal!

A good way of working out whether a restaurant is geared towards tourists or locals is to see when it is at its busiest. Tourists tend to eat a lot earlier than the locals in most foreign countries. Any restaurant that is empty until around 9pm and then fills up is probably frequented by locals.

9.2. Car Rental

When it comes to rental cars the costs can vary widely and it really pays to shop around. Sometimes you will be offered good deals as part of your hotel stay or airfare, consider these as combination deals will also be a lot cheaper than you could get on your own.

Booking car rental when you have reached your destination is normally cheaper than reserving in advance if you have not got a good combination deal.

Make sure that you have suitable insurance, as any accident could make a huge dent in your holiday budget! There are good ways to save money, but insurance is not an area that you should scrimp on.

Always select the smallest car that is suitable for your needs, this will be cheaper and will cost less in gas. There is also a reasonable chance that you will be upgraded for free. If you are feeling bold, it is worth asking at the counter if there is any chance of a free upgrade, you never know your luck!

If you are booking car hire from a distance, look at the costs of car hire from the airport as well as from the city that you are staying in. Car hire companies will pay more to have an airport franchise and you may find this reflected in the prices that you are quoted.

Always fill up the gas before you get back to the car rental office. Car rental companies will charge well over the odds for any extra gas that they need to replace on your behalf so take the time to tank up before you get back if you do not want a large bill at the end.

10. BUDGET TRAVEL WITH A FAMILY

Traveling as a family can really add to the costs. Children are often charged a lot more than seems fair and the overall price of a family holiday can soon get out of hand by the time you factor in all of the food and activities.

10.1. Family Camps

An increasingly popular choice for families is the family camp. Accommodation varies with everything from a basic tent to well equipped log cabins with all of the modern facilities that you would expect in a large hotel.

YMCA offer a range of camps such as the Snow Mountain Ranch in Colorado that spans 5,100 acres and can host 2,500 people in cabins. Activities are available for children aged 3 and over including skiing, climbing and riding. Adults can enjoy use of the gym and health centre or simply enjoy a bit of quiet time while the children are being tired out!

10.2. Money Saving Booking Tips

When you are booking with children it is really important to get to know what deals are available. Some companies offer children's prices right up to 16 years old, others start to charge full price at age 3. Depending on the age of your children, one company may prove substantially cheaper for the same holiday.

Consider your sleeping arrangements carefully. Some hotels will offer adjoining rooms, others will have family rooms that sleep children as well as adults. Most hotels will not allow young children in their own room, so bear this in mind when booking.

If you have more than two children you may find that an apartment offers better value for money and more usable space. A two or three bedroom cottage will often be a lot cheaper than two or three rooms in a hotel.

Use the children as a means of negotiation. For example, ask for a discount on their air fare or accommodation or ask for free entrance to an activity while you are booking.

10.3. Keeping a Lid on Spending Money

Traveling with children can be expensive when you add up the costs of activities, food and children's clubs if they are available. If you are working to a budget then it may well be worth considering an all-inclusive holiday resort. Although these are normally more expensive to book initially, it is easier to anticipate your spending in advance. As meals and drinks are included you will not have to worry about the constant demands from the children for soda!

Find out how much children's clubs will cost and when they are available, prices can vary substantially, so do your homework if you are not to get stung with a large bill at the end of the holiday.

It may even be worth traveling with another family with children of a similar age, as the adults can then take it in turns to child mind, meaning that everyone gets a break and the children have friends to play with! Also the bigger the group the bigger the discounts, normally, so even if you do not want to spend the whole time with another family, you can still benefit from booking together.

CONCLUSION

Finding a bargain holiday is all about being aware of the market and the deals that are available. Pay attention to the basics such as when you are going to travel or where you want to travel. If you can be a bit different to the masses you will find that you can make huge savings.

Plan in advance and join as many reward programs as you can so that you can be made aware of upcoming deals and benefit from long term savings.

Consider shopping online and using auction sites as well as waiting to the last minute, if you are not fussy about destination. Alternatively, using the online consolidators will give you an excellent idea of the prices that are currently on offer.

Being aware of what you can get gives you a hugely advantageous bargaining point. Just remember, you are the customer, so ask for what you want, and don't be afraid to haggle.

DISCLAIMER

All of these tips are accurate at the time of going to press. Please be aware, however, that the travel industry is very dynamic and things can change very quickly. Following the advice in this book does not guarantee that you will get a low cost holiday and those planning a cheap vacation should do their own research to ensure that they get the best possible deal for their individual circumstances.

9 786069 837146

Printed by Libri Plureos GmbH in Hamburg,
Germany